The Ultimate Guide To:

Small Talk!

Quickly Overcome Shyness And Social Anxiety, And Talk To Anyone With These Proven Communication Skills!

Ryan Cooper

STOP!!! Before you read any further....Would you like to know the Secrets of Transforming your life, overcome insecurities, develop leadership skills, and undeniable confidence in your personal, professional, and relationship life?

If your answer is yes, then you are not alone. Thousands of people are looking for the secret to have unstoppable confidence and self-driven power in all areas of their lives.

If you have been searching for these answers without much luck, you're in the right place!

Not only will you gain incredible insight in this book, but because I want to make sure to give you as much value as possible, right now for a limited time you can get full **100% FREE access to a VIP bonus EBook** entitled **LIMITLESS ENERGY!**

Just Go Here For Free Instant Access:

www.PotentialRise.com

Legal Notice

Disclaimer Notice

information contained herein on the new conditions whenever they see applicable.

Table Of Contents

Introduction

I want to thank you and congratulate you for purchasing the book, *"Small Talk: The Ultimate Guide To Small Talk! - Quickly Overcome Shyness And Social Anxiety, And Talk To Anyone With These Proven Communication Skills!"*

This book on "Small Talk" contains proven steps and strategies on how to overcome shyness, social anxiety, or even moderate discomfort when speaking to strangers!

You will never know how greatly someone can benefit your life or how you can benefit theirs in some way if you don't speak to them! You might meet a special someone....Or just imagine the new friends you could have if you just simply talk to people when you are in public! Also, consider the advantages that you would have professionally if you weren't afraid to spark up a conversation with strangers.

If you have ever felt shy about talking to other people or even just being in other people's presence, then you are not alone. Many people feel uncomfortable with having to strike up conversations, especially if they have to do so with strangers. There are those who would prefer to keep to themselves and even those who would consciously try to avoid being with others as much as possible.

However, being human is as much about being social beings as it is about breathing, eating and sleeping. That is, for one reason or another, you will have to face other people, mingle with them and participate in conversations properly.

Thanks again for purchasing this book, I hope you enjoy it!

Chapter 1: Shyness And How To Overcome It

Shyness is not something to be ashamed of. As funny as that may sound, everyone undergoes this feeling of shyness in one way or another. Do you remember the time when you had to stand in front of the whole class to introduce yourself? Or that time when you had to be in front of your boss and other business partners so that you could deliver your report? How about that moment when you had to give a speech on your best friend's wedding or on your parents' anniversary?

Even when you just meet people for the first time, it is not uncommon to have a feeling of uneasiness that keeps you from saying the right things or that keeps you wanting to run away as fast and as far as possible. You feel nervous and anxious, and all you could do is wish that you had never been in that situation in the first place.

Many people have the misconception that only introverted people experience shyness. Introverts, after all, are known for avoiding social situations because they often prefer to be with themselves rather than with other people, but it is very different from having the feeling of shyness. On the contrary, shyness is that tendency to feel tense or awkward and sometimes even worried during social encounters. Most of the time, this feeling of unease is associated with social interactions with strangers, but it can also happen in different situations.

It is said that shyness can be observed through certain symptoms. Some people who are shy can easily blush when faced with an awkward moment. For others, shyness brings with it sweating, the quick pounding of the heart and even the feeling of an upset stomach. There are also times when shyness sets off less physical manifestations such as that of the person who is shy as having negative feelings about themselves. People who are shy tend to worry about how other people will look at them or how other people see them, and thus they would rather withdraw from social interactions than to have to worry about other people's perception of them.

Following these facts, it is not easy to find that everyone undergoes shyness at least at one point in their lives. Even the most confident person can feel shy about meeting the person of his or her dreams, and even more so towards meeting that person's parents and other family members. A well-established businessman would also feel anxious when it comes to dealing with new partners or perhaps when it comes to addressing the shareholders, despite the fact that he or she is already very much respected and looked up upon. And even the world's greatest leaders would probably stumble and falter when given unexpected praises or comments.

Again, there is nothing to be ashamed of when it comes to being shy. It comes naturally just as much as breathing is naturally a part of being alive. However, if you find yourself feeling shy and you know that the shyness is keeping you from doing what you must, then there is something that has to be done. The good thing is, there are more ways of overcoming shyness than you may think.

Feelings of shyness often come from being too self-conscious or from being overly worried about what other people may think. In some cases, this can lead to awkward social moments where the shy person stutters or finds it hard to maintain eye contact or any level of physical contact, but in other worst cases, it can also lead to intense social phobia. The most common occurrences of shyness are associated with interactions with authority figures such as teachers, bosses, and leaders, with romantic interests and also with various group settings.

Overcoming Shyness

Those who wish to overcome their shyness should put utmost importance into understanding what their shyness is all about. Take note that this is not just about understanding what shyness is, but more about having a clearer idea about what their personal shyness truly is.

Each person experiences shyness in a unique way. The cause for shyness varies, the signs and symptoms also differ, but most importantly, the source or the reason for shyness is also different from one person to another. Before you can go on trying to overcome your shyness, you should have a deeper understanding of what it is all about and where it stems from. By knowing the source, you have a much better chance of addressing the issue from its root and therefore get more favorable results from overcoming shyness.

There are three main reasons why people tend to feel shyness. The first of these is a weak self-image. When you see yourself as someone who is never enough or someone who always does the wrong things, chances are that you will always be anxious around other people. Unfortunately, how you think about yourself or what you see yourself doing is often manifested into the real world. This means that if you believe that you will do something wrong, you most probably will.

However, this also means that the solution is very simple – stop thinking so negatively about yourself! This is easier said than done, but it is one of the most fundamental ways of how you can overcome shyness. Remember that a weak self-image is just a voice inside your head. But that voice is your mind and what you are thinking. Tell that voice to shut up or better yet, make that voice say the opposite of the negative things that you are thinking.

The second main reason why people tend to feel shy is because they are too conscious of how they may come off to other people. It may only be natural for human beings to be conscious of what other people may be thinking about them, but to be unable to function properly as a result of this is never a good thing. Those who are shy because of this reason will spend hours and hours preparing themselves so that they look good in front of other people.

Even so, they will always be conscious about every move they make and whether or not they are turning other people off. The simple solution to this is to not focus on one's self too much. Other people are probably thinking of other things besides you anyway, so you should do the same thing.

Finally, people also tend to become shy because other people actually think that they are shy. When you are labeled as being shy, there is a greater tendency to actually experience shyness in social situations. Even if that person being labeled as shy is willing to overcome the label, the problem is that those who have labeled them will still treat them as such. Then again, this is all just a matter of perception. So what if other people think that you are shy? The more that others think this way, the greater the reason you have for proving them otherwise.

All of these reasons have their own validity, but the simple fact is that you have to get over these thoughts if you want to overcome shyness. Stop thinking negatively about yourself, do not stress yourself too much about what other people may think and actually get over what other people think of you. Overcoming shyness starts with accepting that you are shy, understanding why that is so, and having a conscious effort of turning things around.

Chapter 2: Social Anxiety And How To Stop Feeling Anxious In Social Environments

It is not hard to see how feelings of shyness can turn into social anxiety. When one is socially anxious, he or she is overly self-conscious at times of social situations. This leads to difficulty in interacting with other people, and oftentimes this also leads to avoiding speaking with other people as much as possible. Social anxiety also results to having the feeling of being negatively judged by other people and as a result, much like with shy people, the reaction is simply to avoid social environments as much as they can.

Like shyness, social anxiety or more formally known as social anxiety disorder is very common around the world. Millions of people suffer from fears of social situations every day. There are those who get distressed over being introduced to someone new, being the center of attention, or even just being watched while in the process of doing something. Emotional distress can also come from being teased or criticized, from having to deal with authority figures, or from simple personal interactions such as with friends and family members. When these awkward situations occur, the person with social anxiety may be overtaken by a feeling of fear that is manifested through rapid heartbeats, blushing or turning red, trembling, sweating, dryness in the throat or mouth and muscle twitching especially around the face and neck.

Getting over such feelings of anxiety may not be easy, but it is not impossible either. While the third-party observer might simply say that you have to face your fears head-on, it can take more than that. After all, before you can face your fears, you have to be prepared and armed so that you will not succumb to it.

One of the best ways to stop yourself from feeling anxious is to simply let yourself be more relaxed. Simple breathing exercises will do the trick for you. Start with breathing deeply, inhaling and exhaling every couple of seconds or so. It will also help to count along or to breathe along with a mantra that could help you calm your nerves.

You see, social anxiety is much like shyness in that it stems from negative thoughts and beliefs. Those who suffer from social anxiety are afraid that they may end up doing something foolish or that people will think they have nothing to say. It might not be easy to do but the next step to overcoming social anxiety is getting over such negative notions. Think about what you are thinking and actively question them. Are you really worrying about something that is likely to happen, or is it just worthless worrying? Is what you fear rational? Does it make sense? Questioning all of your worries do not even have to lead to an answer, but they will lead you to thinking that maybe you are truly worrying over nothing.

Knowing this, you can now move on to calming yourself by thinking about other things and avoiding your negative thoughts. Some people may find it helpful to visualize peaceful settings that could help them overcome anxiety: a walk in the park, gentle waves that caress the shore, or even a soft breeze as it brushes over the hilltops. These thoughts can help you feel more at ease as they will keep your mind off the negative ideas and also give you something positive and reinforcing. The next step would be to move your thoughts on to something else.

People who are anxious are worried about what might happen or what they think could happen. So why not stop worrying about the future? Think of the present and engage yourself in the now if you want to avoid being anxious. If you are starting out, avoid thinking deep thoughts as well so that you can lighten your mood as much as possible. It will also help to be an observer rather than focusing your thoughts on yourself and being overly conscious, you can be more aware of the other things happening around you.

For example, look at what other people are wearing. Is the food being served delicious? Or perhaps you can keep yourself preoccupied with simple tasks such as fixing your things. Focus on anything but yourself, and ideally, turn your thoughts into things that you actually like and enjoy. Make yourself as relaxed as possible because the truth is that no one is out to get you.

Never think that avoiding social situations is the answer to solving your anxiety problems. In fact, avoidance could only lead to your anxiety becoming worse. What you can do to prepare yourself is to actually practice what you could do during such situations. In most cases, people with social anxiety disorders undergo therapies that help them develop their communication skills. Practice talking with other people because this is what is most likely to happen in a social situation. If you are more comfortable doing so on a one-on-one basis, go ahead and do it. If you find yourself scrambling for words to say, start off by reading from a book or any random form of writing.

Being anxious will not simply go away. You have to face the fear head-on, and the best way to do so is to prepare yourself by actually practicing what you have to do. You can work on your communication skills, attend social skills classes, or you can even do volunteer works for causes that you feel strongly about. And of course, you have to make yourself feel calmed and at ease. Being comfortable is one of the keys to stopping yourself from feeling social anxiety.

Chapter 3: Social Skills And How To Develop Good Social Skills

Social skills are definitely important when it comes to overcoming shyness and social anxiety. These skills are necessary for creating and maintaining relationships with other human beings, and are often defined as the ability to adjust one's behavior in order to fit a particular situation. This involves the way we interact and communicate, whether through verbal or non-verbal means, as well as how we manifest our thoughts and feelings to other people.

While many may think that the extroverted and exuberant style of interacting with others is the most ideal type of social skill, it is not the best and only way to efficiently relate to others. Even people who are shy or introverted can develop a good set of social skills that will allow them to create and maintain successful interpersonal relationships that can have far-reaching consequences in one's life.

Social skills are developed early on in a person's life. As children, human beings often interact with others by copying the examples being set before them. It is very often that how parents and older relatives act are the way that children will also act in their lives. For example, parents who are polite tend to have children who will also be respectful.

On the other hand, children who grow around adults who often curse will most probably pick up the habit and learn to curse as well. This is very important to take note of because many parents leave the teaching part to the daycare or to the school, but the truth of the matter is that they will always be the first teachers that their children will have. That being said, if you want your child to develop good social skills, you should teach him or her by example.

Children naturally develop social skills by themselves, but there are those who need proper coaching so that they do not have to struggle with forming relationships. It should also not come as a surprise that the way children interact is not exactly what parents would expect of them. Sure, the ideal is for children to get to know each other and to play with one another, thus developing friendships, but there are also instances of teasing, bullying, or kids simply being too shy to interact with the other kids.

One of the best ways for children to develop good social skills is for them to be exposed to healthy interactions. This is why children who grow up with other children often find it easier to foster relationships with others. Those who do not grow up with people of their age however, will need guidance from those who are older. If you want your child to develop good social skills, you should constantly speak to them and make them comfortable with human interactions. Start with simple conversations such as asking them how their day went, or if they learned anything new at school.

It is also best to ask a child about the things that he or she likes. Early on, a child will learn how to interact well with others, and by bringing to light their personal interests, they will find confidence and have a positive outlook about themselves. The important thing is for parents to do things with their children and to give them positive reinforcements.

Of course, not all children grow up to develop good social skills. Those who turn out to be shy or anxious in social situations find it more difficult to interact well with others, but it does not mean that they will have to go through such stress their whole lives. Especially for teenagers, human beings will naturally learn and feel that social interactions are an important part of human life. This is why feelings of shyness and anxiety should be overcome as much as possible.

As with children, the best way to develop social skills for any human being of any age is by engaging with others. Easier said than done, people should actively seek out human interaction so that they may develop their social skills, as well as the relationships that they have. Get yourself involved in conversations, be they with persons you are comfortable with or even total strangers.

If you feel anxious about doing so, try to practice what to say on your own. Think about simple conversation pieces even when you are by yourself and think of how you should best react to certain situations. For example, if a friend asked you to hang out, imagine how you could best give a positive response. More than just thinking about what to say, you should even practice actually saying out loud the words so that you have more confidence that you can do it for real when the time comes.

Self-esteem is very crucial for developing good social skills. Develop this by knowing more about yourself and by discovering the things that you are good at. The best way to gain self-esteem is to go out there and show people what you have. After all, there is no better boost to self-esteem than the positive affirmation from others.

Chapter 4: Talking To Anyone And Feeling Comfortable

Once you have developed a good set of social skills, you should find yourself comfortable with talking to anyone and that includes both friends and strangers. As you may have concluded by now, having self-confidence is essential to being able to do so. Being comfortable with other people, feeling at ease when interacting with others, all stem from the feeling of being comfortable about one's self. After all, how can you be comfortable around other people when you are not comfortable with being yourself?

Those who have high levels of self-confidence are the ones who feel positive about themselves. Take note that being self-confident does not have to mean that you think very highly of yourself, but simply that you have a positive view of who you are, of what you do, and therefore, you are not ashamed to show those parts of yourself to other people.

If you want to be able to talk to anyone and be comfortable about it, you should start by letting yourself be relaxed. Avoid feeling anxious or pressured because of what might happen and what other people might think of you. Instead, open yourself up and let your mind wander to more positive thoughts rather than anxieties. Remember that what you think and how you feel can often be sensed by those around you as well.

By opening your thoughts and mind to the positive things around you, you also gain an air of being approachable. People will see that you are not so guarded nor overly conscious and this will allow them to open up to you by themselves. The ability to talk with other people does not mean that you have to be the one to start the conversation, but rather, you have to be open to one so that you can have a positive interaction with those around you.

Another way to feel comfortable when talking with other people is to shift your focus on them and not yourself. Those who are good conversationalists can easily participate in hour-long conversations with minimal talking by letting the other person open up and speak up more. By doing so, they appear to be genuinely thoughtful and at the same time, they have less to worry about because they have less to say.

Remember though that a conversation should be a back-and-forth communication or a give-and-take situation and ideally, participants should have equal moments of talking and listening. Keep this idea in mind and try to focus on the person you are talking with. Ask them things about themselves such as how their day went or what they thought of the show that you just watched, but think before you ask.

Generally speaking, the questions you are appropriately allowed to ask depend on your relationship with the person you are speaking with. This should also dictate your tone of voice and even your choice of words. Even if turning the question towards the other person is a good way to let them know that you are genuinely interested in having a conversation with them, it can easily be a turn off if you end up asking the wrong questions. In fact, one wrong question can turn a perfectly good conversation into an awkward situation.

Chapter 5: Conversation Skills And How To Apply Them

It is easier to feel comfortable with conversations when one is able to apply the skills and tricks of conversing with others. Conversing is a skill and this means that it can be learned and it can be improved with practice and by acquiring new information.

Conversation skills involve knowing what to say and what not to say, how to say them, and when to say them. One of the best tricks of conversation is the ability to praise others. Compliment the way the other person looks or how they have done something perfectly. You can also praise them for the ideas that they have or the positive input they provide. Regardless of what type of praise you give to the person you are interacting with, the important thing is for you to deliver the praise with sincerity and honesty.

Another skill that you should have is the ability to make fun of or to see the fun in yourself. Of all the people involved in the situation you are in, you are the one that you know much about. This means that if you want to make lighthearted jokes about someone, you should make ones about yourself. Also, no one else would be better at making jokes about you than yourself. The best part is that you do not have to get offended because it was your idea in the first place. Even if other people were the ones to point out a joke about you, you should know how to accept the joke and keep the whole situation light and happy for everyone.

In connection with this, you should also avoid making fun of others especially if it is to criticize them or to lower their self-esteem. It is never a good idea to be condescending or to bully other people be they with words or actions. Even if you say such things as jokes, chances are that you will offend someone and no one wants that.

Another skill that is very helpful when it comes to having

conversations is being able to listen to what others say. Many people fret over what to say and how to deliver their lines, but perhaps more important than being able to say things, a good conversationalist should be able to listen well to what others have to say. Turn your attention to the one who is talking. Maintain eye-contact if necessary, and make affirmative gestures that show that you are listening.

One's body language tells much about what that person thinks and therefore, you should be conscious of this as well. Simple nods and smiling at the person who is talking are positive signs, but rolling one's eyes, sighing unnecessarily and even turning away are signs that you are bored and can therefore turn off the person you are talking to.

When you listen in on a conversation, you should also take the next step and actually respond to the things being said. Laugh at jokes, show empathy and share your ideas or simply be patient and not turn your attention elsewhere. If you want to share your two cent's worth, you should know how to time it properly. Do not be too hasty as to cut off other people when they are talking. Also, make comments that are directly related to the topic and conversation to show that you care about what the other person is talking about. A good conversationalist will know to remember the important parts of a conversation so that they can use it as a part of their response or reaction.

A good conversationalist is able to remember and notice many things. Again, this is related to the fact that the focus of one's attention should not be on the self, but on other people and the things going on around them. By being aware of such things, they are able to offer interesting thoughts and insights, and they can also take the time to actually think about what to say before they say it. It is already difficult to know what to say, so if you say something, be sure that you will not regret it.

Of course, a good conversationalist is also one who knows how to speak clearly and slowly. Think of what you want to say first so that you are able to choose the best words. It is also important that you finalize your train of thought first so that your speech does not leave on a hanging note. If you need time to think about what to say, simply speak slowly. This gives you more time to think of what to say next, and it will also make your voice and your words clearer. Stuttering and using fillers such as 'um' should also be avoided as this shows that you are quite unsure of what you have to say. Again, believe in what you say and have the self-confidence to stand by it.

If there are skills that you should have in order to be a good conversationalist, there are also things that you should avoid. One of these is the act of asking too many questions. It is good to focus on others and listen to what they have to say by asking the right questions, but asking too much can turn people off. Asking too many questions may lead them to think that you do not believe what they have to say.

More often, asking too many questions can also say that you actually have nothing to contribute to the conversation. Instead of asking too many questions, mix them with your personal inputs to keep the conversation going. Of course, do not ask questions that do not have anything to do with the conversation either.

Hogging the spotlight is also another mistake that many people make, the pressure of having to speak and becoming the focus of other people's attention can cause many to hog the spotlight for themselves. However, a good conversationalist is able to transfer the focus on other people and other things as well. This not only makes the conversation more interesting, but also, it helps everyone have the chance to speak their own minds.

Chapter 6: Sparking Up Conversations

Starting conversations can be one of the most difficult and challenging things to do. To make it easier for you, try to think of a script or a flow for what you are about to say. The easiest way is to begin by introducing yourself. This is of course in cases where there are new acquaintances involved. Introduce yourself clearly and with a smile and a handshake to make more of an impression. See to it that you are presentable and neat because as they say, first impressions last.

After introducing yourself, you should try to spark up the conversation by using some of these safe but interesting topics. Depending on where you are or if there is any occasion, you can comment on things that you find interesting. Point out facts or comments about the location or any interesting piece that you may find in the venue.

Another trick to keep the conversation flowing is to use open-ended questions. As with the previous tips mentioned, try to focus on the other person or the surrounding instead of yourself. You can ask about the other person's interests, what they think of the latest songs or movies, or what their opinion is of the things going on.

You can also carry light conversations by commenting on the various items that you see. You can compliment on the accessories that they wear or the shoes or bag that they are using. Follow up with positive reactions as well so that you keep the other person interested.

There are also topics for small talk that you can keep in mind. These topics include your hobbies, stories about your family members or even your pets, and of course, about anything you have in common with the other person.

Remember that an important key is to listen carefully and intently so that you can give positive and timely reactions. Talking with someone can be daunting at first, but once you get the conversation started, ease into it and feel relaxed so that you both end up happy and thankful that you found one another in such a situation.

Conclusion

Thank you again for purchasing this book on "Small Talk" and speaking to anyone confidently!

I am extremely excited to pass this information along to you, and I am so happy that you now have read and can hopefully implement these strategies going forward.

I hope this book was able to help you understand how you too can spark up conversations and gain new friends and business contacts.

The next step is to get started using this information and to hopefully live a much more fulfilling life with all the new people you will meet!

If you know of anyone else that could benefit from the information presented here please inform them of this book.

Finally, if you enjoyed this book and feel it has added value to your life in any way, please take the time to share your thoughts and post a review on Amazon. It'd be greatly appreciated!

Thank you and good luck!

Preview Of:

The Ultimate Guide To:

Communication Skills!

Improve Self Confidence, Leadership, And Charisma To Persuade And Influence People!

Introduction

I want to thank you and congratulate you for purchasing the book, *"Communication Skills: The Ultimate Guide To Communication Skills! - Improve Self Confidence, Leadership, And Charisma To Persuade And Influence People!"*.

This "Communication Skills" book contains proven steps and strategies on how to become a more effective communicator, leader, and listener!

In writing this book I decided I wanted to help people to not only become a fantastic communicator and great leader, but I also think it is equally important to become more self confident and to gain skills to persuade and influence people!

In this book's seven simple chapters, you will learn a lot about practical communication skills that you have to master in order to be the best communicator that you can be.

Thanks again for purchasing this book, I hope you enjoy it!

Chapter 1 - Body Language And Communication Skills

Have you ever found yourself in a situation wherein you do not believe what another person is saying to you? Have you ever found yourself not believing that the person speaking to you has enough credibility to say what he is saying? Perhaps, you have found nodding physically but deep inside, your mind is shouting "No!"

The big difference between what a person says and the way we get their message is determined by the speaker's body language marked by the non-verbal cues and signals that they are using. Once you become more aware of these signals, cues, and signs, you will have an edge when it comes to understanding other people and developing your own communication skills.

Sometimes, we encounter situations wherein the subtle and the not-so-subtle signals affect our overall understanding of a message that has been conveyed. These signals usually consist of facial expressions, body movements, gestures, and the shirts in the body posture. The way a person sits, talks, and walks tell a lot about their message because these are reflections of what's going on inside their heads.

In order to become a better communicator yourself, you need to have a better understanding of the body language. This will help you become more aware with the way you choose to communicate. At the same time, you will learn to read what's on other people's minds. To increase your understanding of what other people are truly saying, you also need to become aware of the signals you are personally sending through your own body language.

Note that there are common signs and signals that you have to be aware of. These usually determine whether the person or the message (or both) are worth believing. The following are some of the things that you have to look out for whenever you communicate (note that the "communicator" can be yourself or other people):

> *) The communicator's posture: A credible person usually stands tall. His shoulders are always leaning towards the back to avoid curved impression.

> *) The communicator's eye contact: This tells a lot about the communicator's sincerity. A communicator who has a good intent usually is confident of looking in the other party's eye. Eye contact usually greatly complements a smiling face.

> *) The communicator's gestures with his arms and hands: A good and credible communicator moves his arms and hands in a purposeful and deliberate manner.

> *) The communicator's speech: A good communicator never leaves anything to doubt. Usually, a confident communicator delivers his speech clearly and slowly.

> *) Tone of the voice: A good communicator keeps the tone of his voice as low as possible. The lower the tone, the more confident and more serious he seems.

Aside from decoding other peoples' body language and signals, an understanding of these elements are truly useful in effectively communicating what you have to say to other people. The knowledge of body language will help you send emotions, feelings, and intent that you want your audience to see. This way, you can create a better impression.

For instance, when you are about to enter a communication situation, of course you want to appear that you are a person of sufficient authority on the subject matter. Of course, you also want to show everyone how confident you are of what you are about to say. By controlling your gestures, posture, tone of voice, among others, you can send all the "confidence signals" despite the fact that deep inside, butterflies are flying in your stomach.

Body language has a great impact in the way you deal with others and in the manner you choose to communicate. They are taken to reflect what's happening deep inside your mind, body, and emotion.

Aside from those mentioned earlier, body language includes leg movements, muscle tension, skin coloring (for example, becoming white faced or flushed red), perspiration rate, and the rate of breathing.

These signals may also vary across cultures. Different nations have different kinds of norms and traditions that have to be carefully accounted for. When you try to get to know a person, these should be included in what you are asking and verifying.

Thanks for Previewing My Exciting Book Entitled:

"Communication Skills: Improve Self Confidence, Leadership, And Charisma To Persuade And Influence People!"

To purchase this book, simply go to the Amazon Kindle store and simply search:

"COMMUNICATION SKILLS"

Then just scroll down until you see my book. You will know it is mine because you will see my name "Ryan Cooper" underneath the title.

Alternatively, you can visit my author page on Amazon to see this book and other work I have done. Thanks so much, and please don't forget your free bonuses

DON'T LEAVE YET! - YOUR FREE BONUSES ARE BELOW!

Free Bonus Offer: Get Free Access To The PotentialRise.com VIP Newsletter!

Once you enter your email address you will immediately get free access to this awesome newsletter!

But wait, right now if you join now for free you will also get free access to the "LIMITLESS ENERGY" free EBook!

To claim both your FREE VIP NEWSLETTER MEMBERSHIP and your FREE BONUS Ebook on LIMITLESS ENERGY!

Just Go To:

www.PotentialRise.com

www.ingramcontent.com/pod-product-compliance
Lightning Source LLC
Chambersburg PA
CBHW072030190526
45166CB00015B/1743